Animals Growing Up™

How Seals Grow Up

Linda Bozzo

Enslow Publishing
101 W. 23rd Street
Suite 240
New York, NY 10011
USA
enslow.com

WORDS TO KNOW

blubber A layer of fat under the skin of a seal.

carnivores Animals that eat meat.

cow A female seal.

herds Groups of seals.

mating Coming together to have babies.

predators Animals that kill and eat other animals to live.

pup A baby seal.

species A group of the same kind of living thing that have the same scientific name.

waterproof Not able to get wet.

CONTENTS

WORDS TO KNOW 2
SEAL SPECIES 4
GIVING BIRTH 6
WELCOME, PUPS! 8
SWIMMER SEALS 10
NO BLUBBER 12
FEEDING ON FISH 14
CRYING PUPS 16
FUR COAT 18
LOOK OUT! 20
EXPLORE 22
LEARN MORE 24
INDEX 24

SEAL SPECIES

There are many different **species**, or kinds, of seals. Some species form large groups. These groups are often called **herds**. Seals can be found in most waters of the world.

FAST FACT

The southern elephant seal is the largest seal in the world.

A herd of southern elephant seals rests on a beach.

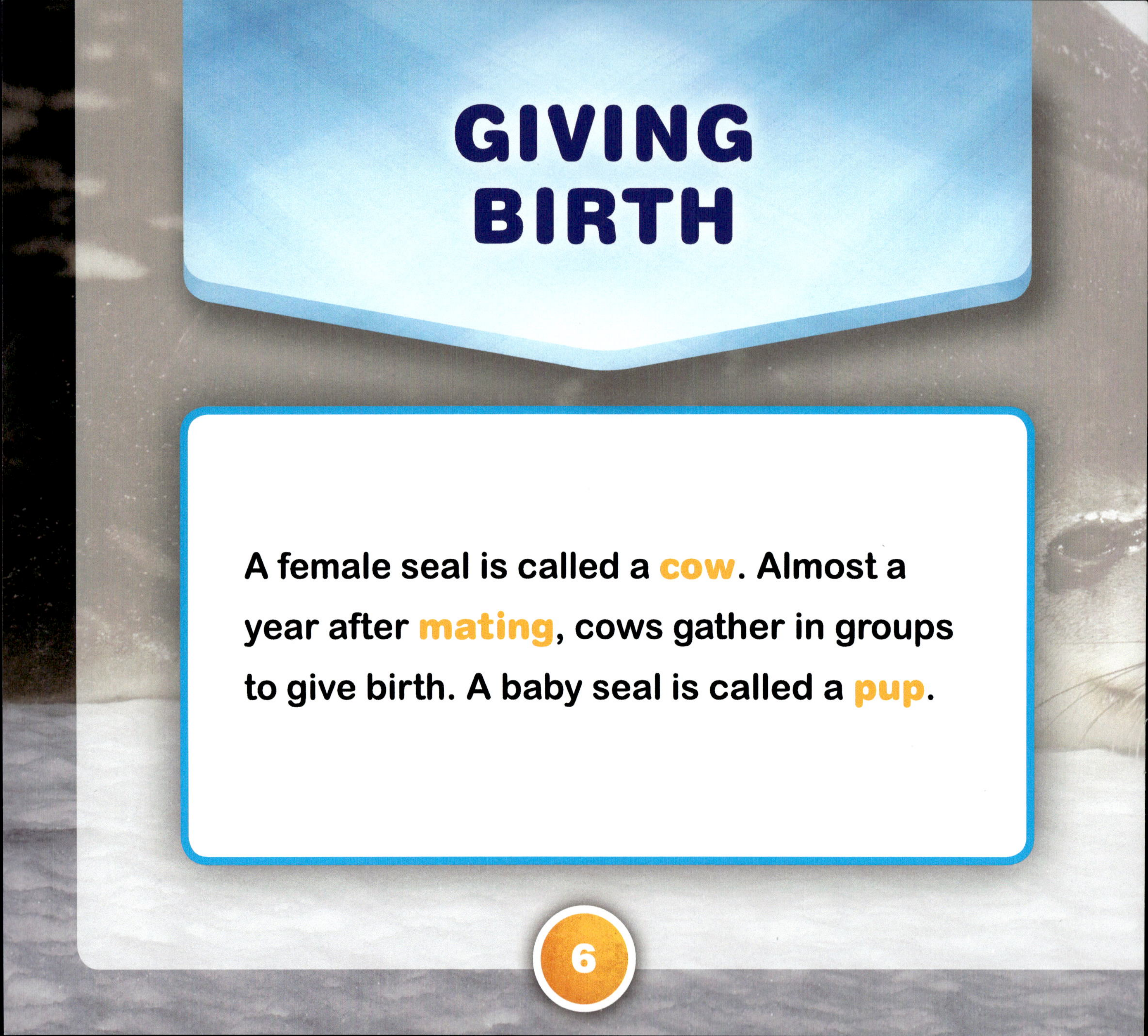

GIVING BIRTH

A female seal is called a **cow**. Almost a year after **mating**, cows gather in groups to give birth. A baby seal is called a **pup**.

A ringed seal cow cuddles with her pup in the snow.

FAST FACT

Cows give birth to a single pup once a year.

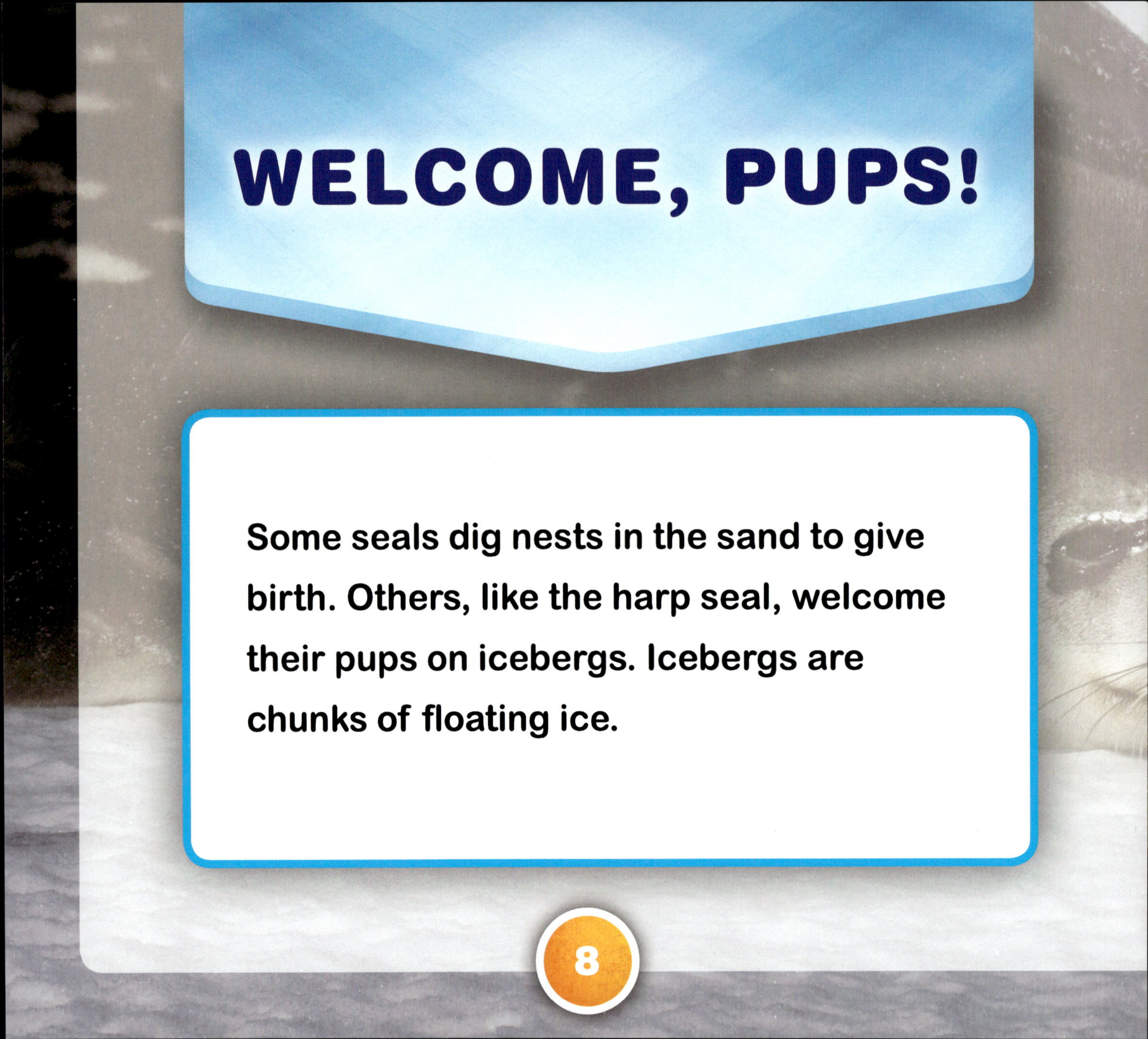

WELCOME, PUPS!

Some seals dig nests in the sand to give birth. Others, like the harp seal, welcome their pups on icebergs. Icebergs are chunks of floating ice.

FAST FACT

A cow can tell it's her pup by its smell.

A harp seal pup lies in the snow in Canada.

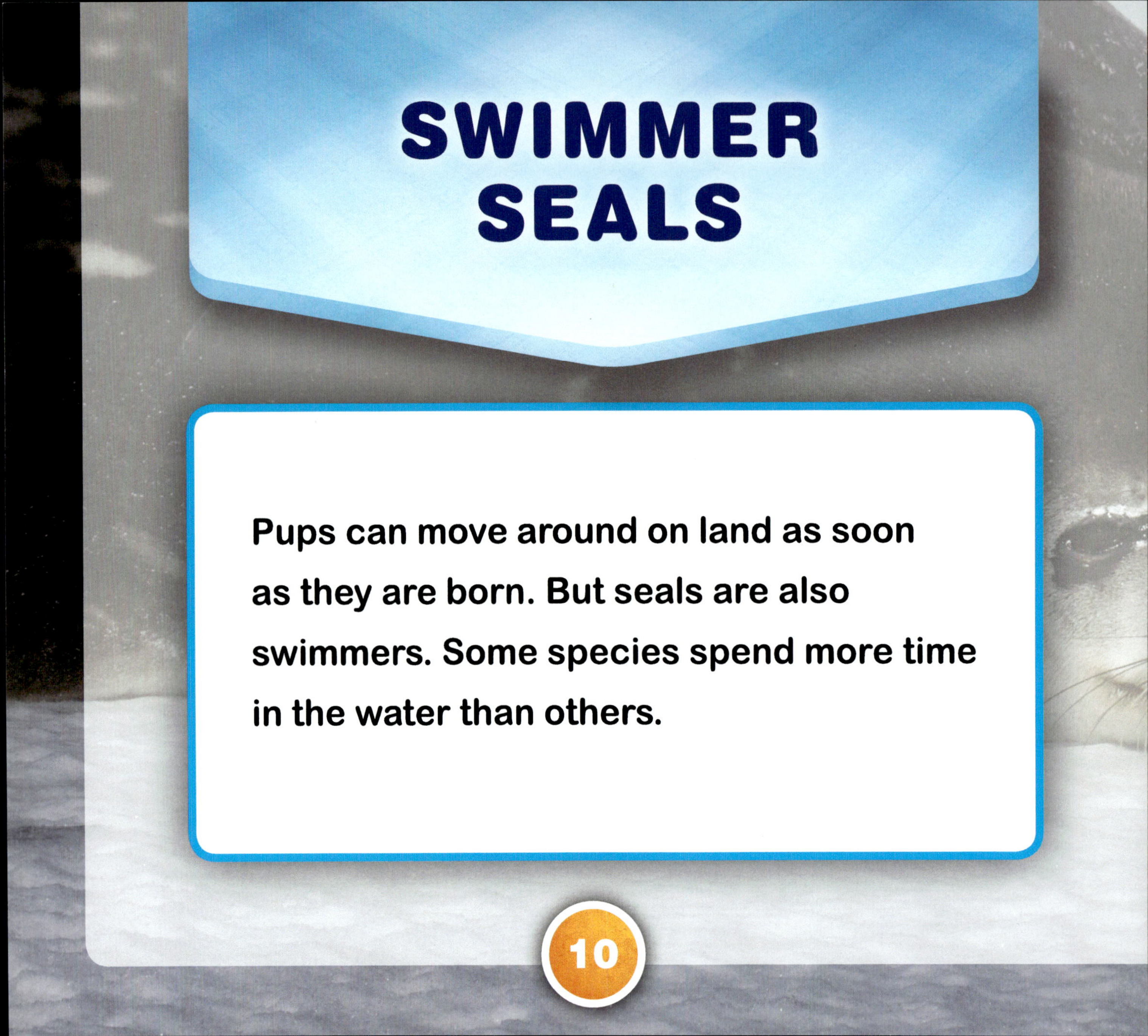

SWIMMER SEALS

Pups can move around on land as soon as they are born. But seals are also swimmers. Some species spend more time in the water than others.

FAST FACT

Some seals will sleep underwater.

A seal pup can learn to swim soon after it is born.

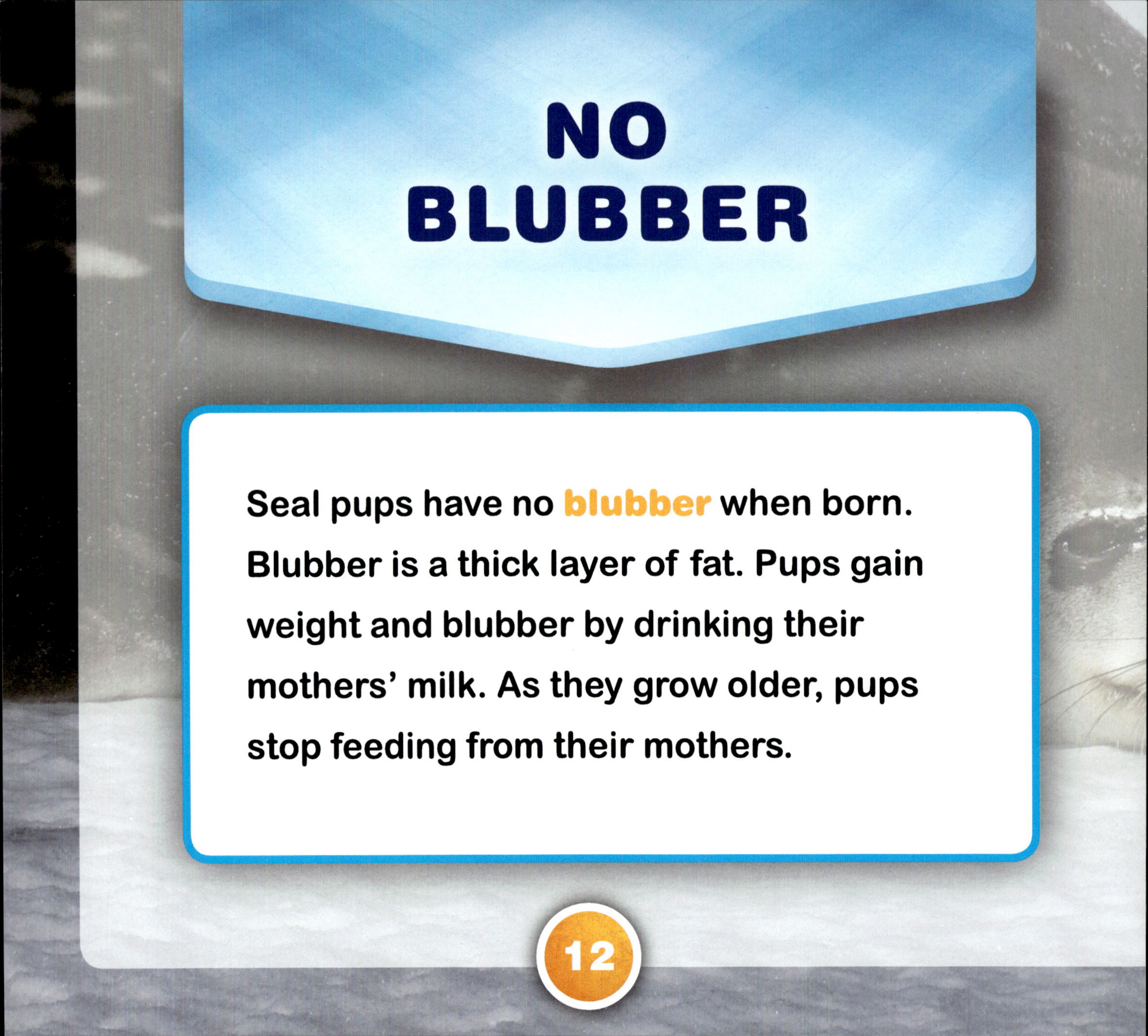

NO BLUBBER

Seal pups have no **blubber** when born. Blubber is a thick layer of fat. Pups gain weight and blubber by drinking their mothers' milk. As they grow older, pups stop feeding from their mothers.

FAST FACT

Blubber helps keep seals warm in cold waters.

A harp seal pup drinks milk from its mother. It has to get fat to keep warm.

FEEDING ON FISH

All seals are **carnivores**. This means they eat other animals. Most seals feed on all kinds of fish. Each seal species enjoys a slightly different diet.

FAST FACT

Seals do not chew their food. They will either swallow it whole or use their sharp teeth to tear it apart.

A seal pup eats a fish it caught.

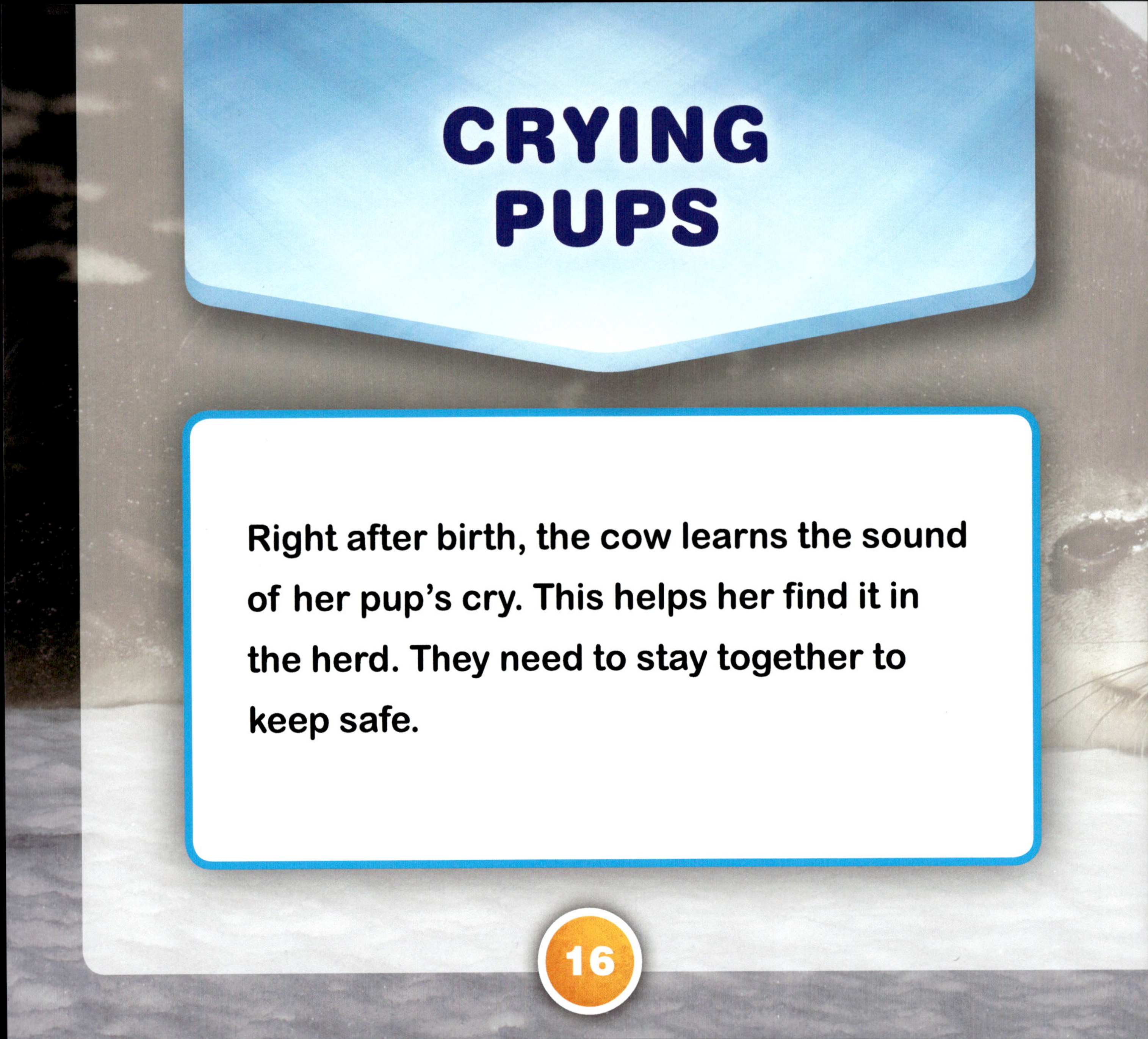

CRYING PUPS

Right after birth, the cow learns the sound of her pup's cry. This helps her find it in the herd. They need to stay together to keep safe.

FAST FACT

A harbor seal's cry can sound like "Maaa!"

A harp seal pup cries for its mother.

FUR COAT

Seal pups can live where it is very cold. They stay on land until their **waterproof** fur coat grows in. This can take around a month.

A harp seal pup's white fur helps it blend into its snowy home. This keeps it safe from other animals.

FAST FACT

As a pup grows, its fur will change color.

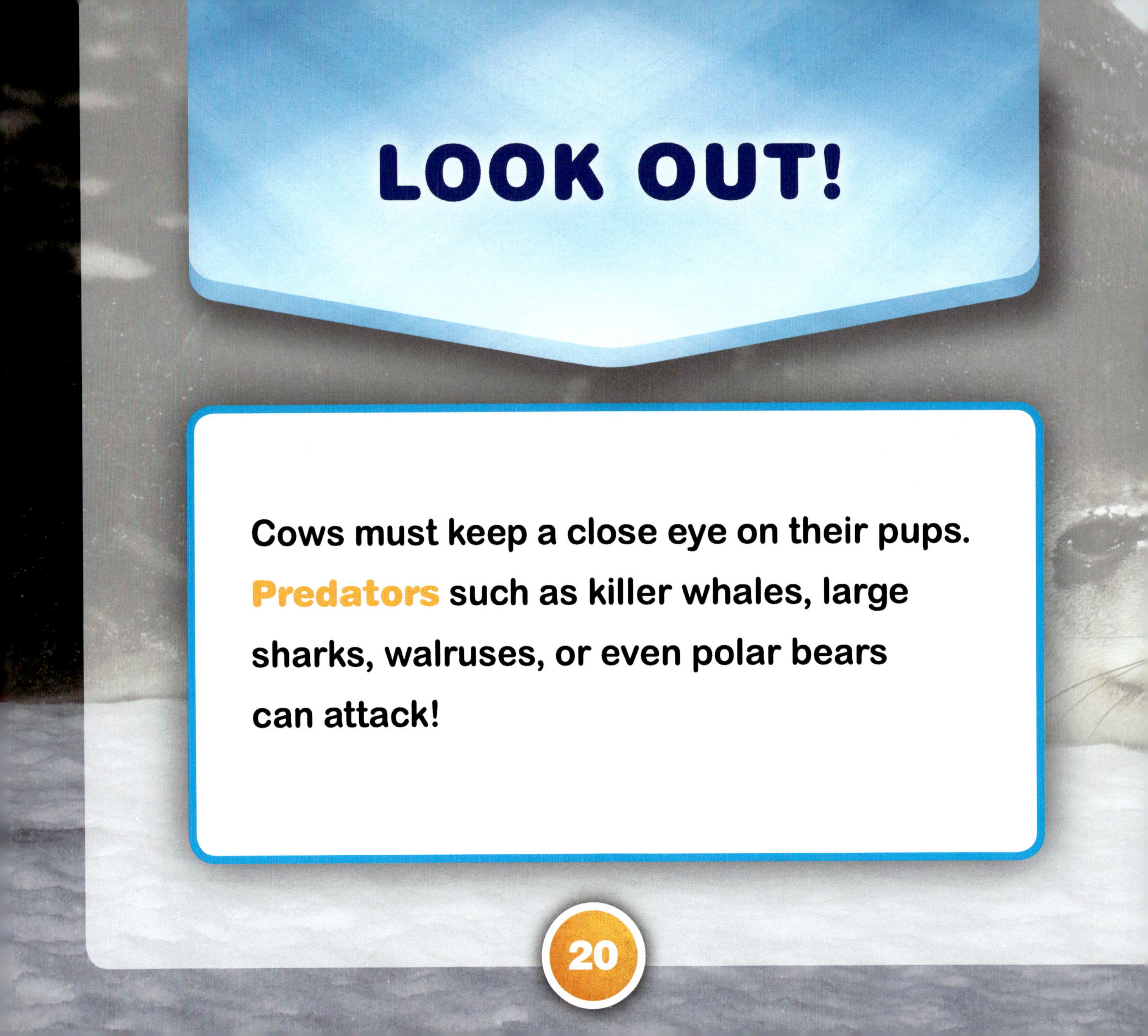

LOOK OUT!

Cows must keep a close eye on their pups. **Predators** such as killer whales, large sharks, walruses, or even polar bears can attack!

FAST FACT

Many species of seals have no natural predators because of where they live and their large size.

A mother seal stays close to her pup to protect it as they swim.

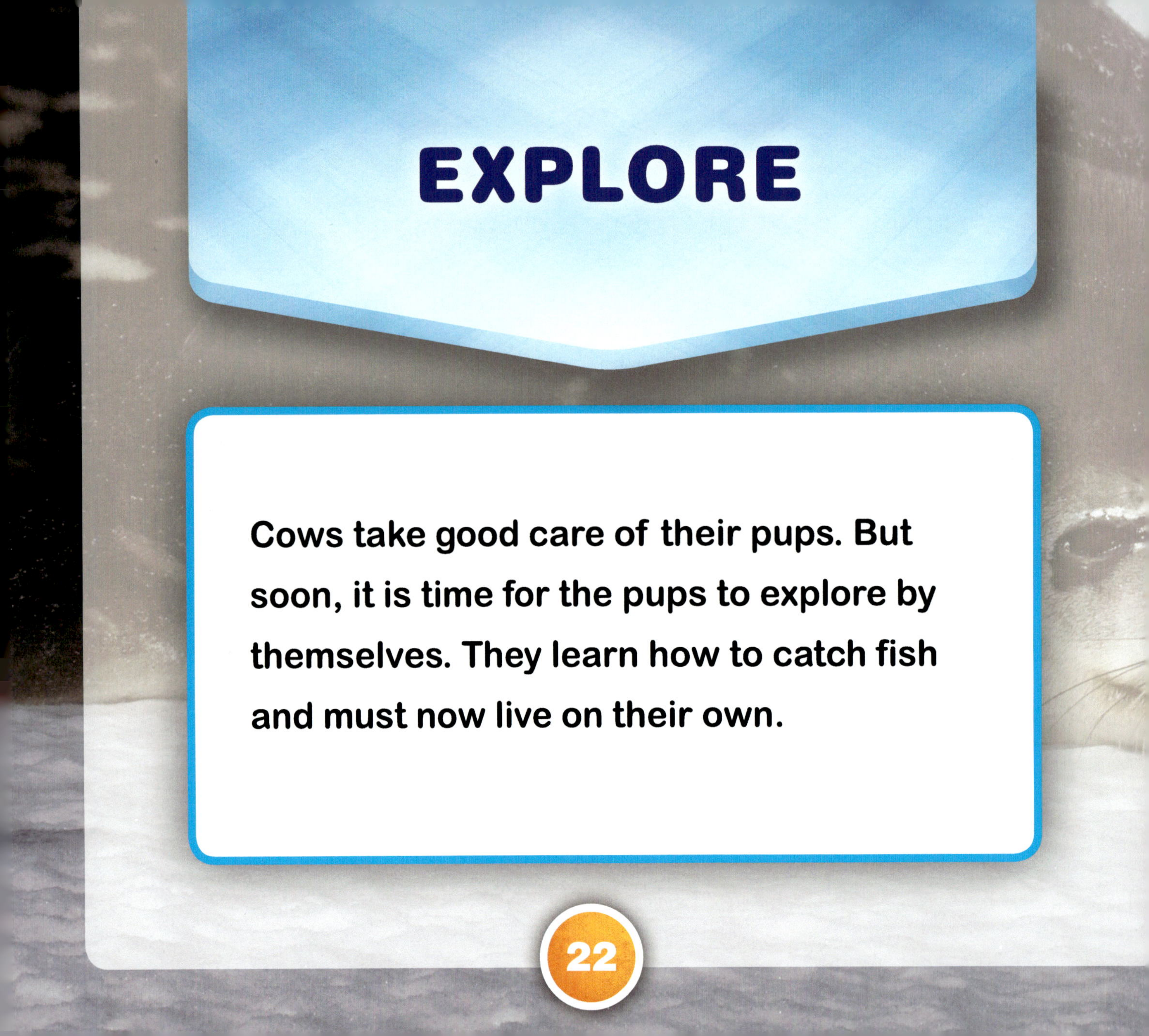

EXPLORE

Cows take good care of their pups. But soon, it is time for the pups to explore by themselves. They learn how to catch fish and must now live on their own.

A gray seal pup must survive on its own at about three weeks old.

FAST FACT

Depending on the species, seals can live 25 to 30 years in the wild.

LEARN MORE

Books

Brannon, Cecelia. *Baby Seals at the Zoo*. New York, NY: Enslow Publishing, 2016.

King, Aven. *Harp Seals*. New York, NY: PowerKids Press, 2016.

Statts, Leo. *Seals*. Minneapolis, MN: Abdo Zoom, 2016.

Websites

National Geographic Kids: Harp Seal
kids.nationalgeographic.com/animals/harp-seal/
Get the facts on harp seals!

Seal Sitters
sealsitters.org/marine_mammals/kidstuff.html
Find fun facts about harbor seals, activity coloring pages, videos, and more.

INDEX

birth, 6, 7, 8
blubber, 12, 13
carnivores, 14
cow, 6, 7, 9, 16, 20, 22
cry, 16, 17
eating, 14, 15
fish, 14, 22
fur, 18, 19
herds, 4
life span, 23
mating, 6
milk, 12
on their own, 22
predators, 20, 21
safety, 16, 20
smell, 9
southern elephant seal, 5
species, 4, 10
swimming, 10

Published in 2020 by Enslow Publishing, LLC.
101 W. 23rd Street, Suite 240, New York, NY 10011

Library of Congress Cataloging-in-Publication Data

Names: Bozzo, Linda, author.
Title: How seals grow up / Linda Bozzo.
Description: New York : Enslow Publishing, 2020. | Series: Animals growing up | Audience: K to Grade 3. | Includes bibliographical references and index.
Identifiers: LCCN 2018046446| ISBN 9781978507227 (library bound) | ISBN 9781978508286 (paperback) | ISBN 9781978508293 (6 pack)
Subjects: LCSH: Seals—Development—Juvenile literature. | Seals—Infancy—Juvenile literature.
Classification: LCC QL737.P64 B695 2020 | DDC 599.79—dc23
LC record available at https://lccn.loc.gov/2018046446

Printed in the United States of America

Photo Credits: Cover, p. 1, interior pages 4–23 (background), p. 7 (main photo) polarman/Shutterstock.com; p. 5 JeremyRichards/Shutterstock.com; p. 9 Jeff Foott/Discovery Channel Images/Getty Images; p. 11 Axel Heimken/DPA/Getty Images; p. 13 Vladimir Melnik/Shutterstock.com; p. 15 Chantal de Bruijne/Shutterstock.com; p. 17 Fred Bruemmer/Photolibrary/Getty Images; p. 19 Enrique Aguirre/Shutterstock.com; p. 21 Anneka/Shutterstock.com; p. 23 Nicram Sabod/Shutterstock.com; back cover and additional interior pages background graphic 13Imagery/Shutterstock.com.